HANNAH UNHINGED

A GUIDED BIBLE STUDY FOR TEENS

SHERREE G. FUNK

© Copyright 2017 by Sherree G. Funk. All rights reserved.
Published by Serving One Lord Resources, Sewickley, Pennsylvania

Unless otherwise noted, all Scriptures are taken from the *Holy Bible, New International-al Version, NIV.* Copyright © 1973,1978,1984 by Biblica, Inc. used by permission of Zondervan. All rights reserved worldwide. Www.zondervan.com

ISBN 978-0-9823137-7-0

DEDICATION

Dedicated to all praying mothers

and all children suffering from abuse or bullying.

Acknowledgments

I wish to thank all the girls --Emma, Josi, Rachel, Reyna, Christy, Kyalie, and their friends -- who helped me refine this study when we first used it at Ingomar Church in August 2015. I will always love these great young women. I expect their faith will blossom and they will be blessings to those around them all their lives.

Many thanks to Megan Delgrosso, Youth Director at Ingomar, and Laurie Hollenbeck and Danielle Seitz for their support and encouragement in these bible studies.

Without the assistance and tutelage of Mark Gulden I might never have learned how to use InDesign to typeset this book.

Thanks also to my wonderful husband Jim for his patience and prodding. It has taken a long time to finish this. And to all my family and friends who make life full and fun, Grazie!

My heart is full of gratitude to the great God of all the universe, who loves us through every storm, hears our every prayer, and won't ever let us go.

Hannah Unhinged

CONTENTS

Week One:	*Faith Through Pain*	*1Samuel 1:1-2*	11
Week Two:	*Taunted and Teased*	*1Samuel 1:6-7*	21
Week Three:	*Spiritual Fruit for the Journey*	*1Samuel 1: 3-8*	31
Week Four:	*Hannah's Heart Unhinged*	*1Samuel 1: 9-18*	39
Week Five:	*Hannah At Peace*	*1Samuel 1:18-28, 1Samuel 2:1-10*	49
Week Six:	*Hearing God's Voice in the Midst of Chaos*	*1Samuel 2: 11-36, 1 Samuel 3:1-10*	59
Week Seven:	*Samuel, Hannah's Godly Son*	*1Samuel 7, 8, 9, 10, 13, 15, 16*	70

FROM THE AUTHOR

Most teens today have experienced bullying, either personally or at close range. They have either felt the pain or they have seen what it does to relationships in families or in schoolyards. Never has the need for this study been greater. Kids need to see how Hannah's desperate heart came unhinged, yet she didn't lose her cool. They need to know God always hears the one who cries out to Him. 'Nowhere to turn' means 'time to turn to God.'

Hannah, the prophet Samuel's mother, had a hard life. Her 'perfect storm' prayer coalesced out of three problem areas: her dysfunctional family situation, her condition of childlessness, and her victimization by nasty bullying. She patiently endured family dysfunction every bit as difficult as what we hear about today. Hannah had no access to self-help books with advice on how to cope with bullying. She had no advanced medical knowledge about her condition and could do nothing to change it. Though she was Elkanah's first wife, she had to play second fiddle to Peninah. But Hannah had one thing more powerful than all that. She knew the same God we know, creator of the Universe, the God who loves us.

If Hannah's troubles are similar to yours, join me in a close look at Hannah's heart - her faith, her patience, and ultimately her peace. Learn how to handle the same kinds of things in your life by pouring out your feelings to God. God will hear your prayers and perhaps use them to change the world.

Message to Students

The Bible is not just for Sunday school or church. When you open it for yourself during a private quiet time, you invite God to speak directly to you through His Word. That is when your own personal journey in discipleship really begins.

To get the most from your study, spend about thirty minutes a day, five days each week. Short on time? Even ten minutes a day will help you.

Some of you may be using this as part of your homeschool curriculum. Others may be doing this with a parent or mentor. Use it however works best for you. Then come together with a small group and discuss your thoughts and findings from the study. Your friends may have found something you missed, or you may give them something to think about.

The important thing is to pray, asking God for understanding and courage to use the principles you learn.

Enjoy your time with Hannah.

Message to Leaders

Choose a regular time to meet: seven sessions of about 90 minutes each. Read the workbook yourself ahead of time.

Locate YouTube videos or recordings of songs from Music Challenges, and consider sharing them with your group.

To help kids be accountable for putting learning into practice, be prepared for the *Reality Challenges*. Assign a "reality checker" to help you.

With younger teens, do the work together in the group session, asking the *Chew On This* questions as you go. In the time you have, select three or four sections to work through and let them finish the rest at home. Then start the next group meeting with the *recap* from the week before.

Thank you for taking time to lead a group of students in Bible study. You are taking seriously the words of Psalm 78:4. "We will tell the next generation the praiseworthy deeds of the Lord, his power and the wonders he has done."

I pray God will bless you richly.

STUDY GUIDE STRUCTURE

This study is designed for use by individuals or groups.

Each week begins with an overview and a prayer to set you off in the right direction. Then five days of study take you deep into the scripture, with simple questions for objective understanding.

Talk About It...

Questions for deeper thought will really get you wondering. There are many possible answers, so get ready to talk about these in your group session.

MUSIC CHALLENGE

Listen To It...
Music suggestions help bring the study into your life. The lyrics are relevant to the week's theme. Find them on iTunes or YouTube.

Act On It...
Hands-on faith challenges will help you put principles into practice.

At the end of each week, a recap section puts all the deeper questions and challenges in one place for group discussion.
The week ends with a prayer.

WEEK ONE
Faith Through Pain

"Don't you see that children are God's best gift? The fruit of the womb his generous legacy?"
-- Psalm 127:3 (The Message)

About 3100 years ago – a very long time – a woman named Hannah married Elkanah, a man she loved. They both worshiped Yahweh, the one true God. Raised in good Jewish families in the area of Ramah, they observed the feasts and journeyed to the temple as required. At that time the temple was more like a tabernacle, or temporary worship center, assembled in Shiloh, a short distance from where the couple lived. The stories of Abraham, Isaac and Jacob were written on their hearts, told again and again in family gatherings. Life was not easy, but God was good.

Though they loved each other, Hannah and Elkanah had problems that seemed to have no good solution. The book of 1 Samuel begins with the story of Hannah. Let's dig in and see what we can learn about a remarkable woman whose faith ran deep.

Dear Lord, take me back to Old Testament times and show me how those stories might relate to me. My problems are surely different from what ancient people faced….. or are they? Maybe we are more similar than I would like to admit. Maybe you never change. Help me see how you helped Hannah. Amen

Day 1: Who's Married to Whom?

Let's begin by taking a look at Hannah's home life. She was married and lived in a town called Ramah. Hannah loved her husband Elkanah, and he loved her. But she still felt a little insecure. Why? Take a look at 1Samuel 1: 1-2. What seems to be the problem?

_____

_____

Hannah had no children with Elkanah. And this may have been the reason Elkanah took another wife, Penninah. Interesting family structure, huh? Do you think Hannah was OK with the multi-wife marriage situation? Why or why not?

_____

Was this what God intended? _____

God made clear his intention for marriage way

back in Genesis 1. One man with one woman, for a lifetime: marriage is a sacred relationship.

What happens in marriage according to Genesis 1:27 and 2:24? _____

_____

_____

Jesus reinforced the idea that marriage is a covenant several times.

Take a quick look at Matthew 19: 3-9. What does Jesus say about divorce? _____

_____

_____

Does he say anything about multiple wives?

Even with these marriage mandates in place, the Biblical narrative includes many prominent characters with multiple wives. It reminds us that God never restricts the choices of his people, even when they lead to less than abundant life.

CHEW ON THIS

Since God defined marriage as between one man and one woman, why did he continue to support men like Abraham and Jacob when they took multiple wives?

God would have been justified in not keeping his promises to Abraham, Isaac and Jacob, since they were always sinning in one way or another. Yet then God might never have had a "people" to call His own.

CHEW ON THIS

Does God's faithfulness carry more weight than our sins?

God's faithfulness to his own promises outweighs every human sin. Humans may not be reliable, but God is always faithful. We can count on that.

Are you in a blended family with siblings from a stepmother or stepfather?

Do you have half-brothers or half-sisters?

How easy is it to get along with everyone?_____

Are you a child of divorced parents and spend alternate weekends in different houses? Do you have friends in this situation?

In what ways is this difficult?_____

REALITY CHALLENGE

What can you do to show love and acceptance to friends in difficult family situations?

Day 2: What, No Babies?

Having a second wife may have been a way for Elkanah to ensure his family line would continue, but it was not God's way. In this story we see Elkanah for what he was: an outwardly spiritual man, who made all the right pilgrimages to the tabernacle, but who took the matter of children into his own hands. We don't know if he prayed about it. He probably didn't. Hannah, though deeply spiritual, had to deal with the reality of the situation. It was hard.

He was not the first Bible character to do this. One thing I love about the Bible is how its writers never leave out the bad parts to make the story sound better. Some pretty big mistakes of God's people are included. Even the embarrassing parts of the Bible have something to teach us.

Hannah felt defective and unlovable. Even today, childlessness sometimes feels like a curse.. You may know someone who has faced this heartbreak. Or you may have to face it yourself one day. According to the American Centers for Disease Control and Prevention, approximately 10% of American women of childbearing age deal with infertility.

Read some anonymous comments from women unable to conceive:

- "I feel left out. I always imagined that one day I would be a mother."
- "I ache. I have no one to talk to about this. It hurts."
- The pain of not conceiving is suffocating and it takes over your whole being. It makes you feel useless as a woman especially when other women are having children. You start to doubt your self-worth.
- The journey of infertility is something people can't see. It's not recognized. It's an absence; it's a dream unfulfilled. It's silent and painful.
- You're stuck in sadness, anger, jealousy, guilt, shame, and depression.

Do you know anyone who has faced the pain of a condition they could not help or change? Perhaps a disability of some kind? How did they handle it?

If you had to deal with such a disability in your family, how would you handle it? Could you trust God with it?

Day Three: Babies R Us

Today surrogate motherhood is accomplished clinically, but in Bible times such a procedure was unheard of. Sometimes other women were summoned to bear a man's children. Naturally, when this happened, feelings surfaced which made the relationships more complicated. When Abraham's wife, Sarah, and Jacob's wife, Rachel, were faced with barrenness they gave up and offered their maids as surrogates. What is a surrogate? Look up 'surrogate mother' in a dictionary or Google it.

Sarah's Story

Abraham's wife Sarah had been barren for years when Abraham heard God's promise that they would have descendants as numerous as sand on the beach.

Read Genesis 12:1-3, and Gen 13:14-16 for God's promises to Abraham.

Now read Genesis 16:1-4a . What did Sarai (Sarah) suggest? _____

_____

_____

Did Abraham hesitate? _____

Did it work? _____

In Genesis 16: 4-6, we see how Sarah felt after this successful surrogate mother gave birth. Why was she upset with Hagar?

_____

So maybe the surrogate solution was a bad idea. It produced a child, but also great family discord. In the end, this was not the child God had promised.

Read Genesis 17:1-2 and 15-22. How old were Abraham and Sarah when Sarah finally became pregnant and gave birth to a son? _____

This son, Isaac, was the child God promised. How do you think Abraham and Sarah felt when God finally gave them a son?

_____

Rachel's Story

Jacob met and fell in love with a beautiful woman named Rachel. Then he worked seven years to gain her hand in marriage. On their wedding night, his father-in-law substituted his other daughter Leah for Rachel. Jacob was more than a little upset, outraged in fact, but agreed to work another seven years for the hand of his true love, Rachel. He ended up with both sisters as his wives. Oh boy. Thus one of the greatest dysfunctional families in the Bible began to take shape. This was only the beginning.

Read Genesis 29:31-35. Who got pregnant first?

Rachel or Leah? _____

How many sons did she have?

____2 ____4 ____6 ____8

Read Genesis 30: 1. Who got jealous?

_____

Keep reading Genesis 30: 2-8. What did Rachel decide to do? _____

How many sons did Bilhah the maid have? _____

To keep things interesting in the sisterly rivalry, what did Leah decide to do in Genesis 30:9-13?

_____

How many sons did Zilpah the maid have?_____

All this sounds crazy enough, but Rachel was still barren. Leah in the end had 6 sons and one daughter and the maids each had 2 sons, so Jacob was father to 10 boys and a girl.

Enough, you say! Well, read Genesis 30: 22-24. Now who gets pregnant?

_____

And what is this son's name?

_____

For a long time, Joseph was the baby of the family, and his father's favorite. We'll talk later about some of the problems caused by this favoritism. But for now, just remember how many extra wives were taken and children born because of Rachel's infertility.

It really highlights how insecurities from not having children were just as real back then as they are today.

Rebekah's Story

Isaac married a girl named Rebekah, who was also barren at first. Genesis 25:21 tells us how these godly parents handled the situation.

What did Isaac do? _____

He prayed. That was a different way to deal. In answer to Isaac's prayer, God blessed Rebekah with twins, Jacob and Esau.

All these stories were written in scripture before Hannah was born. She probably learned them when her own parents passed them down.

What are you dealing with that you have not yet prayed about? Would you try praying about it for three days?

MUSIC CHALLENGE

A song that Hannah might have related to is Come As You Are *by David Crowder. Find it on YouTube or iTunes. Can you think of another song Hannah might have liked?*

Day Four: God's Timing

Many years later, God chose to bless another elderly barren woman with a child. Her name was Elizabeth.

Read Luke 1:5-25 for her story.

To whom did the angel Gabriel first speak?
_____

Why do you think the angel told Zachariah first?

Contrast Elizabeth and Zachariah's reactions to this pregnancy.

_____

_____

What did Elizabeth and Zachariah name their baby in Luke 1:57-64? _____

This man became the prophet known as John the Baptist, the one who prepared the way for Jesus.

How did Elizabeth's response to childlessness differ from Rachel's or Leah's or Sarah's?

_____

_____

Sometimes God chooses to bless us with children later in life. He knows what he is doing even when we can't see it.

When Elizabeth's young cousin, Mary, was pregnant with Jesus, Elizabeth, pregnant at the same time, was a wonderful comfort to Mary! John and his cousin Jesus grew up together.

If Elizabeth had borne children earlier in life, would she have been ready to raise John in the way God intended and would John have known who Jesus was?

Chew on this: Is God's timing usually better than what we plan? Or what we want?

Why is it important to wait patiently for God in all things?

Day Five: Faith Exercises

Hannah lived during the period of the judges. These were rough times. Many Israelites turned away from God and worshiped idols like Baal. Even many of the faithful forgot what God had done in liberating the slaves from Egypt and bringing them into the Promised Land.

Hannah was a religious person. She learned the history of God's people probably from her parents. Which of these stories could she have known?

- ❏ Abraham and Sarah
- ❏ Zechariah and Elizabeth
- ❏ Jacob and his wives
- ❏ Isaac and Rebekah

How might knowing these stories have contributed to Hannah's faith?

_____

_____

_____

Let's go back to the story of Abraham for a minute. God promised to give Abraham descendants as numerous as the stars or grains of sand. But it was hard to believe when he and Sarah had been childless for so long. They both were really too old to have children. But what exactly is faith? Is it believing in the obvious, the real, the possible?

Or is faith more about believing in the unlikely, the not-yet, the unseen, and the impossible? When Abraham believed God, he was choosing to exercise faith. He decided to believe that God could do what he said. And here's the really good part: God counted Abraham's faith as righteousness.

What are some stories about God in the Bible that have contributed to your faith?

_____

_____

Have you seen God's work in today's world? Or in your life especially?

_____

_____

Does that help you have faith for the future?

Faith is not something we can obtain when we want it or need it. Faith is a gift. God surely gave Hannah a large dose of faith to cope with her childlessness. And she chose to exercise it. Somehow Hannah was able to think about a good and merciful God, and she had faith that He could do anything.

The gift of faith grows when we exercise it and it increases when we remember how God has worked in the past.

Keep the faith, Hannah. You're gonna need it!

MUSIC CHALLENGE

Oceans (Where Feet May Fail) is a wonderful song by Hillsong United. Find it on YouTube or iTunes. It speaks of having trust without borders, something I think Hannah must have had.

WEEK ONE RECAP
Faith Through Pain

Learn Anything?

We all have problems. Sometimes we have to live with a condition we wish we could change. Hannah had two problems in 1 Samuel. She couldn't have children and her husband had taken a second wife. Living in a non-traditional family structure is challenging for anyone. Having patience and faith through the hard times requires a lot of prayer. Isn't it amazing that God didn't give up on Bible people who made mistakes in marriage? His promises are more powerful than anyone's errors.

Talk About It...

1. Since God defined marriage as a covenant between one man and one woman, why did he continue to support men like Abraham and Jacob when they took multiple wives?

2. Does God's faithfulness carry more weight than our sins?

3. Do you know anyone who has faced the pain of a condition they could not change? How did they handle it?

4. If you had to deal with a disabiity in your family, how would you handle it? Could you trust God with it?

5. Why is it important to wait patiently for God in all things?

6. Is God's timing usually better than what we plan? Or what we want? Why or why not?

WEEK ONE RECAP
Faith Through Pain

MUSIC CHALLENGE

Listen To It...

Come As You Are -- David Crowder
Oceans (Where Feet May Fail) -- Hillsong United

Reactions:

_____
_____
_____
_____

Act On It...

1. How can you show love and acceptance to friends in difficult family situations?

2. What are you dealing with that you haven't yet prayed about? Try praying about it for three days straight.

Dear God, I want to trust you with everything in my life. I need to remember how you answered Isaac's prayer for Rebekah. I need to remember how you provided a child at the right time to Abraham and Sarah and also to Zechariah and E;izabeth.
When I am tempted to be impatient, Lord, remind me that your timing is always perfect. Amen.

WEEK TWO
Taunted and Teased

"All who see me mock me, they hurl insults, shaking their heads."
— Psalm 22:7

When people look different, sound different, or act differently from those around them, they are often the objects of ridicule. It can happen to a chubby person in a crowd of skinny ones; or a smart person in the company of not-so-bright ones; or a slow-thinker in a crowd of smart-alecs. It could happen to a person with a disability or a genetic condition. It could happen to a Christian among non-believers or a Muslim among Christians. You name it. You have seen this.

Statistics tell us that 70% of students have witnessed bullying.

About 25% of students in grades 6-12 are bullied, many of them physically injured in the process. Studies have shown that victims of bullying often suffer humiliation and insecurity, finding it difficult to make friends and sometimes fearing even going to school. Even in adulthood these effects persist, often leading to depression and other psychological disorders.

Today bullying can be done remotely. Meanness comes through cyberspace too. It hurts just as much.

Dear Lord, at school I see bullies who make life uncomfortable,
even frightening for some kids. It has even happened to me.
Show me what the Bible says about bullying.
Then teach me how to handle it. Amen

Day One: Provoked By a Bully

Besides her inability to have children, and her unconventional family structure, Hannah had a third problem. Not only was she one of Elkanah's two wives, but Peninnah, the 'other wife', was mean to her.

Read 1 Samuel 1:6-7 to discover Hannah's problem. _____

In these two verses, what is Peninnah called? ___
_____

What did Peninnah do to Hannah, year after year? _____
_____

Below, in today's language, are some things which could be included in the general term "provoking."

Have you ever been bullied? Circle things from this list that you have experienced at least once.

teasing   *making fun*   *mocking*

playing pranks   *taunting*   *gossiping*

bullying   *stealing*   *rumor-spreading*

rude comments   *the silent treatment*

exclusion   *spitting*   *threatening harm*

pushing, tripping, pinching, kicking, hair-pulling or other physical abuse

cyber-bullying via social media

If any of this ever provoked you, how did it make you feel?
Circle all feelings that apply:

belittled   *afraid*   *frustrated*   *sad*

insecure   *angry*   *ashamed*   *shy*

self-conscious   *other* _____

I'm sure it didn't feel very good. I remember being teased in school for my name, for my clothes, for being smart. Perhaps that explains my shyness as a teen, and that I was usually very quiet in class.

What were you tempted to do when you were bullied?
_____

What did you actually do about it?
_____

Depending on the severity or frequency, you might be tempted to retaliate. Is that ever a good idea?_____ Why or when?_____
_____

How is self-defense different from retaliation?_____

CHEW ON THIS

What makes people "bully" others? What are some other options or courses of action?

MUSIC CHALLENGE

A recent song that speaks of the power of language is "Words" by Hawk Nelson. Check it out on YouTube and listen.

We used to say, "Sticks and stones can break my bones, but words will never hurt me." Unfortunately it's not really true, is it? Words can hurt a lot.

Day Two: Shoe on the Other Foot?

Now let's turn the tables. Have you ever done any of these things to someone else? Circle them.

teasing   *making fun*   *mocking*

playing pranks   *taunting*   *gossiping*

bullying   *stealing*   *rumor-spreading*

rude comments   *the silent treatment*

exclusion   *spitting*   *threatening harm*

pushing, tripping, pinching, kicking, hair-pulling or other physical abuse

cyber-bullying via social media

Uh-oh. Now we're getting personal. It's easier to talk about other bullies than to admit we've done the same thing. Peninnah bullied Hannah repeatedly. She knew Hannah's infertility made her unhappy and self-conscious. Hannah felt bad, and was no doubt jealous of Peninnah. That single difference, a baby, made Hannah feel inferior, unworthy, and vulnerable to Peninnah's taunts. In Hannah's view of the world, Peninnah had everything while she had nothing.

Instead of helping Hannah, or at least showing some sensitivity to her problem, Peninnah took advantage of the situation, teasing and provoking Hannah while inflating her own ego. We don't know how far she went in her bullying. But I can imagine some sweet comment she might have made when Hannah was within earshot:

> "These children keep me so busy, but they are such a blessing to us. Too bad *you* can't have children, Hannah."

OR

> "Hannah, since you have no children, could you babysit for a while? I need to do some other chores."

OR

> "Oh dear, I'm pregnant again; Hannah, could you please get me a drink of water? I'm just *so* tired."

And every year, on the road to Shiloh, people probably stopped them, remarking to Peninnah how the kids had grown, while Hannah stood by, aching to have children of her own.

What do you think Peninnah hoped to gain from provoking Hannah? _____

How can we keep ourselves from joining in the bullying or teasing of others?

Consider someone you have hurt. Think of how you made that person feel. Can you genuinely apologize and make the effort to show respect and kindness in the future?

Day Three: Other Bible Bullies - Ishmael

The Bible includes stories about plenty of bullies. In Week One we read how Sarah gave her maid, Hagar, to Abraham so he could have a child. Here is another part of that story.

Read Genesis 21:9-10. Who was mocking whom, and why? _____
_____
_____

Is there any group or type of person you have learned it's easy to make fun of? How did you come to believe this?

The story goes back a few years, when Sarah thought the best way to get a son for Abraham was to let her maid, Hagar, get pregnant for her. The two women didn't exactly become BFFs over that. Hagar's son Ishmael picked up his mother's prejudice, rudely mocking Sarah and Isaac. Upset, Sarah sent Hagar and Ishmael into the desert, but God heard their cries. Interestingly, God showed mercy on Ishmael.

What did God do in Genesis 21:17-20?

_____

Can you change your prejudiced opinions? Often prejudice is only destroyed when we deliberately work to change our thoughts toward a group or an individual.

I'm sure Ishmael was sorry for his words, and God showed mercy.

If you have ever teased, mocked, bullied or hurt someone, do you think God can forgive you? Of course he can. Sometimes children take on the prejudices of their parents, acting out in ways they later regret. Be on guard against the temptation to bully or hurt people thinking others will praise or like you for it. Listen to God. He's the only one who matters.

Day Four: Other Bible Bullies - Joseph's Brothers

Ordinary tensions between people can be greatly magnified within families. Sibling rivalry can lead to life-long bitterness between brothers and sisters. Often the situation is the result of parents showing favoritism, sometimes intentionally. Take Joseph for example.

Remember the extended family of Jacob? He had two wives who were sisters: Rachel and Leah. Then each wife had a maid: Bilhah and Zilpah. It turns out Jacob had children by all of them. Can you believe it? Anyway, he always loved Rachel the most. So when her sons Joseph and Benjamin were born, Jacob doted on these sons and the rest were treated to less love and attention. In reality, Joseph may have played up his "favorite son" status, often tattling on his older brothers.

Read Genesis 37:1-4. Is this a classic case of favoritism?_____

Genesis 37:11 describes the cause of the brothers' resentment. What was it?_____

It's not really surprising that his brothers resented Joseph. But what they did when Dad wasn't looking seems extreme.

Read Genesis 37:12-28. Jot down the five sinister plans. Circle the ones they actually carried out.

1.
2.
3.
4.
5.

When everyone feels the same about someone, "groupthink" begins to take over and together they do far worse things to the scapegoat than any one would have done alone. Have you ever seen this happen at school? Or in your family?

What can you do when you see someone becoming a scapegoat?

It may help to change the subject, diverting attention away from the scapegoat. Remember that you are not perfect and perhaps some of the same things you dislike in someone else are in your heart as well. Also remind the others of the good qualities or characteristics of the scapegoat. Remember to think about consequences for your deeds.

The next time you witness bullies, try to do something. Contact an adult who can do something. Say something in defense of the person or something kind to the person. If you see cyber-bullying, make it a point to say, post, or do something to change the situation.

Joseph's misfortunes drove him closer to God. The Bible repeats how God's presence reassured Joseph.

Read each of the following verses and record what God's presence did for Joseph in each case.

Genesis 39:2 _____

Genesis 39:3 _____

Genesis 39:21 _____

Genesis 39:23 _____

Now read how Joseph forgave his brothers and blessed them in Genesis 45:3-11.

Who does Joseph credit for his position of honor after all those years? _____

If you have time, read Joseph's story, full of unbelievable twists and turns, in chapters 37, 39-50 of Genesis.

How does mild bullying sometimes lead to something much worse? Why does this happen? What do you think bullies your age are looking for?

Often bullies are looking for control or power. Sometimes the bully is looking for favor in the eyes of someone. Joseph's brothers craved more attention from their father.

MUSIC CHALLENGE

Listen to the song "Forgiveness" by Matthew West. Do you agree it is the hardest thing to give away?

In hindsight, Joseph recognized God's mercy during his miserable trip to Egypt and his lengthy stay in prison. It may be too early for you to gain Joseph's kind of perspective, but stay close to the Lord, who will grant you His peace, in His timing, as you seek it.

Lamentations 3:22 says, Because of the Lord's great love we are not consumed for his compassions never fail. They are new every morning; great is your faithfulness."

Day Five: Jesus was Bullied, Too

Even Jesus was bullied. Read about Jesus's experience in his hometown of Nazareth shortly after beginning his ministry.

Find it in Luke 4:16-30.

In verses 28-30, what did his neighbors and acquaintances try to do after Jesus delivered his first sermon?_____

Now read Luke 20:20-26.

The religious leaders used entrapment techniques, hoping to catch Jesus saying something they could use to arrest him.

What was the result?_____

In the end, Jesus was betrayed by one of his own disciples. That was pretty hard to take. If you have been betrayed by a friend, know that you are in good company.

When brought before Pilate for questioning, Jesus did not argue his case. We know that Jesus was innocent; He lived a sinless life and he could have defended his innocence. But in Mark 15:3-5, how did he respond to the false accusations?

_____

What can we learn from Jesus' reaction? How is this sometimes a good way to respond to bullying at school? When might it be a bad idea?

Fill in the blanks in three of the following verses to see how Jesus was treated by the soldiers, guards, priests, lawyers, and even other guilty criminals: (Use NIV if possible)

Matthew 26:67-68

"Then they_____and _____. Others _____ him."

Mark 15:29-32

"Those who passed by, hurled _____ at him, shaking their heads and saying…. In the same way the chief priests and teachers of the law _____ among themselves. Those crucified with him also _____ on him."

Luke 22:63-65

"The men who were guarding Jesus began_____and_____him. They_____ him and demanded, 'Prophesy! Who hit you?' And they said _____."

John 19:2-3

"The soldiers twisted together a _____ and put it on his head. They clothed him in a purple robe and went up to him again and again, saying "Hail, king of the Jews!" And they _____ him in the face.

John 19:23-24

"When the soldiers crucified Jesus they _____, dividing them into four parts."

What's remarkable in John 18:19-23 is that when Jesus was slapped on the face by the High Priest's guard, he did not turn his face so the guard could slap him again. Instead Jesus responded, "If I said something wrong, testify as to what is wrong. But if I spoke the truth, why did you strike me?" Jesus not only defended himself with words, He quietly confronted the bully and demanded an answer for his unjust treatment.

If Jesus suffered unfair treatment, it should not surprise us when we experience it. Jesus never said our lives would be smooth sailing if we follow him. It is unlikely that life will be perfect for you, no matter how much faith you have. Yet Jesus offers something to anyone who has ever been taunted, teased, bullied, abused or mistreated.

Read John 16:33 and write it here:

"I have told you these things, so that _____

_____

_____

If you are ever bullied or mistreated, speak up for yourself, get away from the situation, tell an adult who can help, and then pray for God's supernatural ability to forgive.

Let that sink in.

You really can trust Jesus to give you peace, even in the midst of painful troubles. He experienced everything you may go through.

A wonderful verse in Isaiah has given comfort to many who have been unfairly accused and mistreated. Read it and consider how this verse could help anyone who suffers from bullying. Isaiah 54:17 says

"No weapon that is formed against you will prosper; And every tongue that accuses you in judgment you will condemn. This is the heritage of the servants of the Lord, And their vindication is from Me," declares the Lord. (NASB)

WEEK TWO RECAP
Taunted and Teased

Learn Anything?

Bullying hurts. And sometimes we even bully others without thinking. Hannah had problems she could not change and Peninnah used them to provoke her. The Bible has lots of stories like this, and it helps to see that uncaring people even taunted Jesus. Seeing how some people handled the bullying gives us a way to deal with it ourselves. And we can be more aware of our own words and actions so as to be more like Jesus wants us to be.

Talk About It...

1. What makes people bully others? What are some other options or courses of action?

2. How can we keep ourselves from joining in the bullying or teasing of others?

3. Is there any group or type of person you have learned it's easy to make fun of? How did you come to believe this?

4. What can you do when you see someone becoming a scapegoat?

5. How does mild bullying sometimes lead to something much worse? Why does this happen? What do you think bullies your age are looking for?

6. What can we learn from Jesus' reaction to bullying? How is this sometimes a good way to respond to bullying at school? When might it be a bad idea?

WEEK TWO RECAP
Taunted and Teased

MUSIC CHALLENGE

Listen To It...

Words -- Hawk Nelson

Forgiveness -- Matthew West

Reactions:

_____

_____

_____

_____

Act On It...

1. Consider someone you have hurt and genuinely apologize.

2. How can you break the cycle of prejudice? Often prejudice is only destroyed when we deliberately work to change our thoughts toward a group or individual.

3. The next time you witness bullies, try to do something. Contact an adult who can do something. Say something in defense of the person or something kind to the person. If you see cyber-bullying, make it a point to say, post, or do something to change the situation.

4. If you are ever bullied or mistreated, speak up for yourself, get away from the situation, tell an adult who can help, and then pray for God's supernatural ability to forgive.

Dear Lord, I see now that even good people in the Bible were bullied. It is never a good thing. Help me to not be a bully or even to tease or make fun of others. Be with me when I feel afraid and deliver me from harm. Help me forgive others just like you have forgiven me. Amen.

WEEK THREE
Spiritual Fruit for the Journey

"But the fruit of the Spirit is love, joy, peace, patience, kindness, goodness, faithfulness, gentleness, and self-control; against such things there is no law."
— Galatians 5:22-23

As a kid, I both loved and hated family vacations. I loved the National Parks we visited. I hated the drive getting there. I liked looking out the windows on steep mountain roads. But curvy switchbacks made my brother carsick. We kids in the back seat fought about who had to sit in the middle. We didn't have an SUV or station wagon with extra seats. We drew imaginary lines on the seat and screamed when a sibling crossed the line with even a finger. "He's in my space!" "Her head is falling on my shoulder." "He touched me."

One summer we drove clear across America. It was fantastic. But we were on Dad's "itinerary" so we arose every morning at six and drove a couple of hours before breakfast. I didn't like the tight schedule. I wanted more time in a mountain park. Every afternoon we stopped for ice cream. My dad would say, "It breaks the monotony." I unconsciously learned that eating sometimes cures boredom. Maybe that has been more of a problem than I realized.

Family vacations tend to highlight different personalities. So much togetherness can be stressful. What kinds of tensions have you noticed on family trips? _____

_____

This week we start with an annual "family" trip taken by Elkanah, Hannah, and Penninah.

Dear Lord, I know my faith is like a journey. I need help getting started and I need a lot of help along the way. You are my guide. Give me what I need to move forward to what you have planned for me. Amen

Day One: Ancient Vacations

In Old Testament times, God himself had laid out requirements for pilgrimages. The purpose was to remind the people of their great deliverance from slavery in Egypt. It also reinforced the need to worship in a large group. Some of these required trips are described in Deuteronomy 16.

Read Deuteronomy 16: 16-17. How many times a year were the men called to appear before the Lord? _____

List the 'feasts' during which they were to appear before the Lord. _____
_____

And could they show up empty-handed? _____

What were they to bring? _____
_____

According to this passage in Deuteronomy, the festivals would be "at the place God would choose." What does this mean? While the Israelites wandered in the wilderness, they carried a 'tent of meeting' or tabernacle. The tabernacle included a special 'room' in which the ark of the covenant was kept. The top of the ark, called the mercy seat, was literally the place that God met with the people. (Exodus 25:22)

After the Israelites settled in the Promised Land, Joshua set up the tabernacle in Shiloh. (Joshua 18:1) During the period of the Judges the Israelites lacked stable, consistent leadership. The tabernacle remained at Shiloh for more than 350 years. All the annual festivals and daily rituals were done there. After Joshua died, many forgot God, slipping carelessly into worship of other gods in other temples. The events recorded in the book of Judges illustrate the inconsistent observance of God's commands.

Read Judges 21: 25.

What does that tell you about the general feeling for religion during this time? _____
_____

Though tabernacle attendance was required in Hannah's day, the people rarely obeyed.

Now, back to 1 Samuel. What did Elkanah do year after year according to 1 Samuel 1:3-4?
_____

Given the relaxed attitudes of his day, do you think perhaps Elkanah's observance was unusual? _____

Godly observance of the feasts and worship at the Tent of Meeting was not a high priority for everyone. We can assume that Elkanah and his family were more faithful than many of their neighbors. In our day it is still rare for everyone in a neighborhood to attend worship together.

How many of your neighbors or classmates worship God regularly?

_____ a few _____ about half _____ most of them

_____ I don't really know.

If you worship regularly with your family, do you feel like most of your neighbors are just sleeping in on Sunday? _____

Compare how you feel when you see lots of familiar faces at church with how you feel when you don't. How might this affect someone's faith?

Day Two: Eat! You Look Hungry

So picture Elkanah and his family, making their annual journey to Shiloh. Their home in Ramah was located about sixteen miles from Shiloh, which made for about a two day backpack trip. A donkey or two carried the tents, clothes, food and water, but it was a major operation. Everything had to be packed and carried. While walking they had time to ponder their blessings of the year.

Imagine it with me: Elkanah in the lead, greeting other men on the way. Peninnah often nursing a new baby while chasing a toddler. Hannah trailing behind, acutely aware of her childlessness.

Read 1 Samuel 1: 4-8.

What did Elkanah give Hannah each year at the feast? _____

Why might he want to do this?_____

Remember the daily ice cream stops on my family vacations?

In this generosity to Hannah, what was Elkanah communicating to Peninnah? Was he saying he loved Hannah more?

_____

In week two we talked about favoritism in Jacob's family. Because Jacob favored Joseph, the brothers became jealous bullies. Have you ever seen this kind of thing in your family?_____

Could that have been happening with Elkanah's family? How?

_____

Do you think Elkanah really understood Hannah's sorrow? _____

Was his method of showing love effective?

_____

Why do some people see food as the answer to all problems?

When we offer food as an antidote to boredom, it becomes tied to certain emotions. When a toddler gets a cookie to stop crying, the cookie seems like a cure to some sorrow or disappointment. Emotional eating can lead to poor habits like overeating and other problems.

In John 4: 27-34, what did Jesus say when the disciples offered him lunch?

"I have food to eat that you do not know about."

What was this satisfying "food" Jesus was talking about?

_____

Food is not the best thing to satisfy our longings for love. God himself is the best satisfaction. He loves us more than anyone else ever will.

Day Three: Fruits of the Spirit

Hannah is heartbroken.

She is childless in a world where barren women are shunned. She is loved and fattened by an adoring husband while mocked and loathed by a jealous co-wife. What can she do? Her situation seems hopeless. Thankfully, God created us with a spiritual side. He breathes his Holy Spirit into us. God gave Hannah a measure of this Spirit and its fruits.

Hundreds of years later, Paul wrote about the "Fruit of the Spirit." He was talking about the natural qualities that come to a person with the Holy Spirit.

In Galatians 5:22-23, find and list all nine of these qualities.

_____   _____

_____   _____

_____   _____

_____   _____

_____

Which of these qualities did Hannah display in her misery?

_____

You could point to several, but in particular, I think she showed the last three: faithfulness, gentleness, and above all, self-control.

First of all, let's look at faithfulness.

Another word for faithful is dependable. A person who does a job regularly, faithfully, is one who can be trusted, one who is reliable, dependable.

What did Hannah do that showed this kind of faithfulness?

❏ went to Shiloh year after year in spite of Peininah's bulllying

❏ supported her husband in his priestly duties

❏ sometimes stayed home, because she was tired of Peninnah's jabs

❏ fought back in anger

Another aspect of faithfulness is demonstrating faith – being full of faith.

Do you think Hannah was full of faith in God?

How do you think she felt about God?

We will see very soon just how much faith Hannah had.

Day Four: Gentleness, Another Spiritual Fruit

Hannah displayed not only faithfulness, but also gentleness, another fruit of the spirit.

Gentleness flows from an attitude of humility. It is not a cowering, fearful meekness. We are not made gentle by domineering people who bully us into submission.

Rather, the gentle ones see their circumstances as God-ordained and God-redeemed. God knows the situation we face and promises to be with us. He also promises to weave good out of bad. (Romans 8:28) This kind of gentleness can be full of pain, yet full of grace. Gentleness is not the same as weakness.

How do you see Hannah displaying gentleness?

_____

How is gentleness different from self-control?

_____

Look up Proverbs 15:1 and write it here:

_____

If you have experienced bullying in some form, how could you use gentleness?

_____

Martin Luther King Junior used gentleness in his leadership during the Civil Rights movement of the 1960s.

As I write this, it has been over fifty years since the famous "I Have a Dream" speech. In that speech, Dr. King speaks for everyone who has ever been bullied, dismissed, or ridiculed for something they could not change. He spoke longingly for humans to look deeper than color and see what God sees: character. If the Holy Spirit guides us, we can show character like this that rises above petty mockery and senseless violence.

Perhaps violence is the opposite of gentleness.

"A gentle answer turns away wrath, but a harsh word stirs up anger."

Proverbs 15:1

Why is violence not a good response to bullying?

Day Five: Self-Control, Another Spiritual Fruit

Probably the most challenging item, at least for me, on the list of spiritual fruits is self-control. It may be a fruit of the spirit, but self-control sounds like something I have to do myself. I have a lazy streak when it comes to work on my self. As a result I often find myself lacking in this spiritual quality. How about you?

But Hannah seems to have mastered self-control. She didn't rebuff Elkanah when he tried to console her with mounds of food. She didn't retaliate verbally when Peninnah taunted her.

Can you think of a time when you displayed self-control? Was it difficult? Did you pray first?

Here's a little self-control quiz. Score yourself from 1 = low self-control to 5 = most self-control in each of these areas:

❏ saying whatever comes to mind without thinking who it may hurt

❏ doing homework or chores before having fun

❏ eating too much when hungry or just bored

❏ exercising to stay strong and healthy

❏ reacting when provoked or teased

❏ putting other people's needs first

What resulted from Hannah's self-control?

What are some practical tips for exercising self-control? Write them below. Try one or two this week.

She didn't lash out at those around her. She didn't say things she might later regret. Though hard, self-control is a valuable character trait.

WEEK THREE RECAP
Spiritual Fruit for the Journey

Learn Anything?

Hannah found herself in the most difficult situations when traveling with Elkanah and Peninnah on annual trips to the temple. She knew it would be hard, so she packed her "spiritual fruitbasket." Faithfulness, gentleness and self-control are must-haves when facing a bully or any tense situation.

Talk About It...

1. Compare how you feel when you see lots of familiar faces at church with how you feel when you don't. How might this affect someone's faith?

2. Why do some people see food as the answer to all problems?

3. Why is violence not a good response to bullying?

4. Can you share a time when you displayed self-control? Was it difficult? Did you pray first?

WEEK THREE RECAP
Spiritual Fruit for the Journey

MUSIC CHALLENGE

Listen To It...

Mighty to Save -- Hillsong United

Reactions:

_____

_____

_____

Act On It...

1. What are some practical tips for exercising self-control? Try one or two this week.

Dear Lord, please fill me with spiritual fruit: Love, Joy, Peace, Patience, Kindness, Goodness, Faithfulness, Gentleness and Self-control. I need these qualities every day as I journey though life. Amen

WEEK FOUR
Hannah's Heart Unhinged

"The righteous cry out, and the Lord hears them; he delivers them from all their troubles."
— Psalm 34:17

"This is what the Lord says: 'Call to me and I will answer you and tell you great and unsearchable things you do not know.'"
-- Jeremiah 33:2-3

Life gets crazy sometimes. Relationships that once satisfied us seem strewn with problems. School demands more time than we have. Parents and siblings have no time for us. We get cranky. Even the dog fails to notice our pain. What can we do? Cry in the pillow or call a friend? What if our friends are busy or worse, not really our friends? Hannah felt the same way. What did she do? She turned to God in prayer.

The tornado of God's Spirit touched down on the door to Hannah's soul. Her heart broke apart.

> She came unhinged.
>
> She prayed.
>
> God listened.
>
> God answered.

*Dear God, sometimes I don't know where to turn.
People around me don't understand. I feel alone and frustrated. Can I really talk to you about it? Do you really want to know how I feel?
Teach me how to pray, Lord. Amen.*

Day One: Cry Out to the Lord

Hannah was teetering on the brink of collapse. She had held it together through all of Peninnah's provocations. She had graciously accepted the feasts Elkanah offered. She had patiently reviewed, over and over, the stories of God's faithfulness toward the childless women in scripture. Nothing she could say to Elkanah or Peninnah would change her situation.

Where could she go? To whom could she turn? She knew God would listen. Hannah turned to God in the 'perfect storm' of frustration, sadness, and despair.

What is a 'perfect storm?'

A perfect storm is when several big weather systems collide, making the storm much bigger than any one of them. A collision of life storms is the same kind of thing.

Have you ever seen a perfect storm in your life or in someone else's life?

According to 1Samuel 1:9-10, what did Hannah decide to do and where did she go?

_____

The "temple" at this time was actually the tabernacle assembled at Shiloh many years before. God had promised to meet his people in the tabernacle. Only priests were allowed inside. And some priests, while holding the proper credentials by birth (male descendants of Levi) were not as deeply spiritual as you might expect.

It's not clear whether Hannah pushed into the tabernacle to get as close as possible to the place God called "the mercy seat" or if she simply stood near the entrance, feeling God's presence when she needed it most.

Who was seated on a bench beside the doorpost?

_____

And what two things did Hannah do?

_____

Hannah's cry came from the depths of her broken heart. She cried out to God in her misery. Instead of airing her complaints to Elkanah or sympathetic friends she "presented herself before the Lord" in prayer. For Hannah, it meant going to the temple and just letting out her feelings in heartfelt prayer.

Have you ever done this? Have you ever felt completely helpless, broken-hearted, desperate? What were the circumstances?

MUSIC CHALLENGE

Look for a somg called "Blessings" by Laura Story. What if our blessings really do come through teardrops and rain?

I believe God allows some things to happen to us because He knows we will turn to Him. Thank you God for those things. Things that cause us to cry out for God are really blessings in disguise.

A man whose name appears only briefly in Scripture prayed a very short heartfelt prayer. His mother named him Jabez, which rhymes with the Hebrew word for pain, because he had caused her pain in childbirth.

Jabez cried out to the God of Israel:
"Oh, that you would bless me and enlarge my territory! Let your hand be with me, and keep me from harm so that I will be free from pain."

And God granted his request.

--1 Chronicles 4:10

The prayer of Jabez is simple and direct. God loves prayers from your heart.

Below write a simple and direct prayer from your heart to God.

Day Two: Soul-Baring Prayer

One great benefit of knowing God is that he listens to our deepest prayers. Take the story of Jonah and the whale. Jonah knew what God was asking him to do. His response was to run the exact opposite direction. Not until he found himself in the belly of a huge whale did Jonah pray.

Read his prayer in Jonah 2.

He quotes from Psalms 3, 18, 30, 31, 42, 69, 77, 86, 88, and 116. He even mentions a vow. Jonah was truly desperate, and God heard his prayer from the deep.

CHEW ON THIS

Why do you think Jonah prayed using the Psalms?

The book of Psalms is found smack in the center of most Bibles. It is the prayer book within The Book. The Psalms are full of human emotions, often with the same kind of soul-baring honesty as Hannah's prayer.

Read parts of the following four Psalms and notice the similarities in their beginnings.

> Psalm 77:1-2
> Psalm 86: 1-7
> Psalm 88: 1-3
> Psalm 102: 1-2

What did you see in all four?

_____

Did you notice the tone of desperation?

How might you "present yourself before the Lord" if you felt like Hannah?

Here are some ideas:

_____go to a quiet place alone

_____go to a chapel, prayer room or sanctuary

_____go to your bedroom and close the door

_____take a walk

_____open your Bible to the Psalms and start reading

_____write a prayer to God in your private journal

When such moments sneak up on you, be assured that God is looking for you. He wants to hear your cry for help. When Hannah got to the end of her rope, she found God there waiting for her.

Thank God that he finds us in our hurricanes and holds out his strong hand to save us.

MUSIC CHALLENGE

Amy Grant has a song about this closeness to God that comes with tears: "Better than a Hallelujah." Do you feel you can relate to any of the situations in Amy Grant's lyrics?

Third Day has a song called "Cry Out to Jesus." Do you think Hannah could relate?

Day Three: Nazirite Vows

So Hannah prayed through bitter tears by the door of the tabernacle. As she prayed she made a promise to the Lord.

Read 1Samuel 1: 11.

What did Hannah promise to do if God would grant her a son? _____

What is a Nazirite vow?

We have to look at Numbers 6: 1-21, especially verses 1-5. The Nazirite vow described here is for men or women wanting to "separate themselves for the Lord." According to these verses, what would distinguish a Nazirite?

Diet:_____

Hairstyle:_____

How difficult do you think it would be to make this promise for a child even before he or she is born?

_____

For reference, look up a couple other scriptures about people who took Nazirite vows in the Bible. Match the scriptures to the people:

Judges 13:3-7, 24   Paul

Luke 1: 13-15   Samson

Acts 18:18   John the Baptist

Making vows or strong promises to God can be dangerous. Why? Can you think of a situation in which you might make a deal with God? How hard might it be to keep that vow?

Day Four: Misunderstood

Now please read 1 Samuel 1:12-18.

Eli was watching Hannah while she prayed and cried. What did the priest notice that he found unusual? _____

Remember, some priests were not greatly sensitive to spiritual matters; they gained the priestly office by birth into a priestly family.

Eli thought she was drunk!

Perhaps he had never seen a woman so clearly distraught coming to the Lord in heart-wrenching silent prayer. Perhaps other people were beginning to stare as well.

Centuries later, the Holy Spirit descended with a mighty wind upon a group of disciples. It was Pentecost in Jerusalem when Peter and the others were gathered several weeks after Jesus' resurrection. They were praying together and suddenly they spoke in foreign languages they didn't even know.

Read Acts 2:1-13 to see what many of the bystanders surmised.

How was it similar to Eli's assumptions about

Hannah? _____

REALITY CHALLENGE

Try this: The next time you are out in public, try praying for someone you see. Right now I am in a coffee shop and a man just limped by using a cane. He seems young. I am praying for him silently, with my eyes open.

Hannah was totally in "the zone." She was speaking to the Lord, pouring out her soul. She probably didn't care what anyone thought. Nothing could keep her from praying.

Hannah responded to Eli's impatient question.

Notice how she describes herself: "deeply troubled." She also used the words "great anxiety," and "vexation" in verse 16. Her words must have convinced Eli the priest, who suddenly became more sympathetic.

What did Eli say to Hannah?

_____

_____

And what was her humble, respectful response?

_____

CHEW ON THIS

Are you able to pray silently to the Lord even when other people are around? Can you pray when those around you are not praying?

Day Five: Prayer Changes Things

Prayer is a wonderful thing. It is a conversation with the creator of the universe.

We don't simply recite a wish-list to God. We tell him our concerns, our heart-aches, our joys, our sorrows, and we cry out for help. The Holy Spirit even prays for us when we don't know exactly how to pray.

Romans 8:26 says, "…The Spirit helps us in our weakness. We do not know what we ought to pray for, but the Spirit himself intercedes for us through wordless groans."

The next time you feel anxious, vexed, or distressed about something, pour out your heart before God. Ask God to remember your prayer. Tell Him you need his help. Then listen and wait. See if you don't get some real peace from that prayer.

And many times, God, through his Spirit, gives us a reassurance, a new hope, a deep confidence that everything will be OK.

What did Hannah do in verse 18?

_____

Had anything changed?_____

Why do you think Hannah was no longer sad?

_____

Turn back to Week 3 where the fruits of the Spirit are listed. What fruit do you think Hannah enjoyed after this prayer?_____

Like Hannah, we emerge from anguished prayer with a newfound peace, an indescribable feeling, a knowledge that God has heard our prayers. And even though our situation remains unchanged, we are comforted, strengthened, and ready to persevere through the troubles.

MUSIC CHALLENGE

A band called Seventh Time Down has a song called "Just Say Jesus." Google it. When you don't know what to say, just say "Jesus." There is power in his name.

A rich prayer life is like a really good friendship.

Think of your best friend. Your friendship didn't just happen. How long have you been friends? What do you enjoy doing together? Do you sometimes know what your friend is thinking even before he/she speaks? Do you laugh or cry at the same kinds of things?

A real friendship with God grows only through prayer.

It takes time and effort. It starts with learning simple bed-time prayers and rhymes before meals when we are children. We learn the Lord's Prayer and then we slow down to understand what it means. Gradually, we ask God for things and marvel when He gives them. We begin to pray for others, forgetting ourselves. We try to make time every day for prayer or keep a prayer journal. We go to God with our hurts and our blessings. We thank Him more and more. Our days are better if we start them with prayer and we feel unfocused and unsure when we forget to pray. Soon we begin to know God personally, like a really good friend. And we have peace.

Thank you God for offering peace that is beyond understanding through our prayer life.

How is your prayer life? Do you feel God is a whisper away or do you fear he is not listening at all?

Consider spending more time with God in prayer.

What are some practical steps you can take to strengthen your prayer life?

WEEK FOUR RECAP
Hannah's Heart Unhinged

Learn Anything?

The one thing you can ALWAYS do in ANY situation is PRAY. God is listening. He loves to hear his children call out in whatever situation seems hopeless, dangerous, stressful, or painful. He wants to answer and he will. Pouring out all your feelings to God is a way of presenting your true self to him. God is never far away.

Talk About It...

1. Making vows or strong promises to God can be dangerous. Why? Can you think of a situation in which you might make a deal with God? How hard would it be to keep that vow?

2. Are you able to pray silently to the Lord even when other people are around? Can you pray when those around you are not praying?

3 Why do you think Jonah prayed using the Psalms?

4. How might you "present yourself before the Lord" if you felt like Hannah?

5. How is your prayer life? Do you feel God is a whisper away or do you fear he is not listening?

WEEK FOUR RECAP
Hannah's Heart Unhinged

MUSIC CHALLENGE

Listen To It...

Blessings -- Laura Story

Better Than a Hallelujah -- Amy Grant

Cry Out to Jesus -- Third Day

Just Say Jesus - 7th Time Down

Reactions:

_____

_____

_____

_____

Act On It...

1. Write a simple and direct prayer from your heart to God.

2. The next time you are out in public, try thinking a prayer for someone you see.

3. The next time you feel anxious or distressed about something, pour out your heart before God. Tell God you need his help. Then listen and wait. See if you don't get some real peace from that prayer.

4. Consider spending more time with God in prayer. Try keeping a prayer journal or having a prayer partner.

*Lord, I want to get closer to you in prayer. Thank you for finding me
when I am battered by the wind and rain of my personal life storms.
Hold me up, Lord, and give me peace that goes beyond my understanding.
Amen.*

WEEK FIVE
Hannah At Peace

"Be still, and know that I am God." — Psalm46:10a

"And the peace of God, which transcends all understanding, will guard your hearts and your minds in Christ Jesus." -- Philippians 4:7

Following Hannah's temple experience she quietly got up and went home.

But something very real had gripped her soul in her prayer time. Hannah gained a peace she didn't have before. She no longer winced at Peninnah's zingers. God replaced her desperation with a clear assurance that he heard her prayer. She could gather her emotions and return to her troubling home life with Elkannah and Peninnah.

Though her situation remained the same, Hannah changed.

Dear God, I need your peace.
Please answer my deepest prayers in your perfect time. Help me wait patiently
if my situation does not change the way I wish it would. Give me peace anyway. Amen.

Day One: Hurray, God!

Read 1 Samuel 1: 18-20.

What happened in "the course of time." _____

_____

Hurray, God!!! After years of Peninnah's torment, Hannah gets pregnant and has a son with Elkanah. God chose to honor Hannah's heartfelt request.

You might be tempted to conclude from Hannah's story that if you just pour out your soul to God that God will answer right away. Sorry, but that is not always the case.

It is true that God wants to hear from the depths of your heart, and he will always listen and give you what you need. But rest assured that He knows what's best for your life and those around you. One of the things God is perfect about is this: timing. He alone knows when all things are ready.

Why does God answer some prayers and delay on others? Why do some people get what they pray for and others don't?

During a period of my own pain and heartache I kept praying for those that hurt me and for the whole situation to improve. It just lingered. Nothing seemed to change.

Have you ever prayed and it seemed that God didn't hear for a long time, and then one day everything fell into place? Will you thank Him for that now?

Finally I made a big change in direction, because it was the only way I felt any peace. Then everything began to heal. God didn't answer my prayers in the way I expected, but by forcing me to change direction He led me to a new place, a more satisfying service, and a deep peace. In a strange way, I think it was God's way of drawing me closer to him so he could bless me.

Read Isaiah 55: 8-9.

Can you trust that God's thoughts are more than we can understand? His ways are greater and ultimately far better than ours.

Day Two: Dedicating the Child

Read 1Samuel 1:20-23.

Why did Hannah name her son Samuel?

_____

You *know* Hannah loved that baby. Finally the teasing from Peninnah and neighbors stopped. She was a mother at last!

When Elkanah returned to Shiloh each year for service and sacrifice, what did Hannah do?

_____

Why did she not accompany him as usual?

_____

What kind of mother do you think Hannah was? And why?

❏ overprotective

❏ kind and loving

❏ faithful to teach her son to love God

What was Hannah's intent for Samuel after he was weaned? _____

In those days, mothers nursed their babies for as long as three or more years. One reason for this was the lack of refrigeration for milk and mother's milk was always fresh, nutritious, and available.

Hannah had plenty of time to teach her toddler about God's faithfulness. She could tell him the story of her temple prayer and about her promise to dedicate her baby to God's service. One day Samuel would understand what was expected of him.

Now read 1 Samuel 1: 24-28.

So Hannah returned to the temple at Shiloh with her little boy, Samuel. This was probably at least three or four years after her tearful, unhinged prayer. It may have been even longer, because we don't know exactly how long it was before Hannah became pregnant.

What three things did Hannah bring to sacrifice?

_____

_____

_____

And to whom did she and Elkanah bring the boy?

_____

Because it had been a few years, what did Hannah tell Eli?

_____

If you were the parent of this child, the child you had dreamed of and prayed for, would you have been able to leave him at the temple and return home, trusting that he would be properly cared for?

Then what did Hannah say in verse 28?

_____

"I prayed for this child, and the Lord has granted me what I asked. Now I give him to the Lord. For his whole life, he will be given over to the Lord."

What does it tell you about Hannah's faith that she actually took Samuel to Shiloh to serve the Lord his whole life?

_____

_____

What was the first thing Samuel did at Shiloh with his mother by his side? See 1 Samuel 1:28

_____

Were you taught to praise God when you were just a small child?

If so, what was the first song you learned about Jesus or God?

_____

Did you have another favorite song?

_____

When I was a very little girl, I had a wind-up musical teddy bear that played *Jesus Loves Me*. For years I would listen to that as I fell asleep each night.

My heart learned the truth of that before I knew how to walk.

Is it important to teach small children to worship God? Why or why not?

Day Three: Hannah's Song

After worship, Hannah was filled with joy, another fruit of the Spirit.

The misery of her childlessness was replaced with the joy of motherhood by God's grace. Hannah never wavered from her commitment to give Samuel back to the Lord. Now she had accomplished this traumatic 'letting go' by God's grace as well.

So she sang. Her song is a most beautiful prayer.

Read 1 Samuel 2: 1-10.

I've reprinted it below from *The Message* by Eugene Peterson.

Hannah prayed:
I'm bursting with God-news!
I'm walking on air.
I'm laughing at my rivals.
I'm dancing my salvation.

Nothing and no one is holy like God,
no rock mountain like our God.
Don't dare talk pretentiously—
not a word of boasting, ever!
For God knows what's going on.
He takes the measure of everything that happens.
The weapons of the strong are smashed to pieces,
while the weak are infused with fresh strength.
The well-fed are out begging in the streets for crusts,
while the hungry are getting second helpings.
The barren woman has a houseful of children,
while the mother of many is bereft.

God brings death and God brings life,
brings down to the grave and raises up.
God brings poverty and God brings wealth;
he lowers, he also lifts up.
He puts poor people on their feet again;
he rekindles burned-out lives with fresh hope,
Restoring dignity and respect to their lives—
a place in the sun!

For the very structures of earth are God's;
he has laid out his operations on a firm foundation.
He protectively cares for his faithful friends, step by step,
but leaves the wicked to stumble in the dark.
No one makes it in this life by sheer muscle!
God's enemies will be blasted out of the sky,
crashed in a heap and burned.
God will set things right all over the earth,
he'll give strength to his king,
he'll set his anointed on top of the world!

How do you feel when you have fulfilled a promise? How do you describe the feeling you get when with God's help you have done exactly what you set out to do?

MUSIC CHALLENGE

What is your favorite happy song? There's an old song I just love called "Walking on Sunshine." It just makes me happy. Or maybe you like something newer like "Happy" by Pharrell Williams.

Over the years I have come to know a wonderful feeling, sort of a combination of peace and joy. It comes to me at odd times. My spirit smiles, my entire body relaxes, yet I feel ready for anything. I get a sense that even if things are hard, God is on his throne, casting grace all across his creation. At those times, I feel no stress at all.

The earth is the Lord's and everything in it!!!
Psalm 24:1

I imagine the Christian martyrs of old felt something like this as they were being persecuted. It is a feeling of no anxiety, of being right with God.

Perhaps that's how Hannah felt.

Read 1Samuel 2:1-10 again.

Hannah's song is bursting with joy, but also with something else. Which of the following themes appear throughout?

❏ God is just

❏ God is vengeful

❏ God is powerful

❏ God sometimes reverses the natural order of things

How does this contribute to joy?

MUSIC CHALLENGE

Choose a song that would express your feelings if God answered your deepest prayer. One suggestion is "Thank You, Jesus," by Hillsong United.

Day Four: Mary's Magnificat

Hundreds of years later another mother sang a prayer song much like Hannah's. In fact she may have used Hannah's song as her inspiration.

Read Luke 1: 46-55.

This song is known as The Magnificat. It is what Mary sang while at her cousin Elizabeth's house when the baby in her womb moved for the first time. That baby, of course, was Jesus.

Find at least 3 similarities between the songs of Hannah and Mary.

1._____

2._____

3._____

Both women rejoice at what God has done for them.

They are thankful.

They praise God's ability to turn things around – to bring down the mighty and raise up the humble.

They notice how God hears and helps those who serve him faithfully.

Both women love God without reservation. They rejoice even though their blessings come with difficulties.

The next time you are filled with joy and gratitude over God's blessings, sing your favorite happy song!
Tell people why you are happy.
Give God the credit.

Day Five: Promise of Peace

No matter what drives you to bare your soul to God, He promises to deliver peace.

He gives peace in a different way. It is like a calm assurance, a hush in your soul, a bandage around a broken heart.

No one who claims God's peace has a perfect life. Trouble shows itself in many, many ways in this life. Yet the process of praying from the heart is like wrapping yourself up as a gift to the Lord. He loves it. And you will feel God's peace as you rest in him.

The Old Testament prophet Isaiah knew about peace:

- *Isaiah 26:3 "You will keep in perfect peace those whose minds are steadfast, because they trust in you."*

- *Isaiah 26:12 "Lord, you establish peace for us; all that we have accomplished you have done for us."*

- *Isaiah 32:17 "The fruit of that righteousness will be peace; its effect will be quietness and confidence forever."*

Jesus also talked about peace.

- *Luke 24:36 "While they were still talking about this, Jesus himself stood among them and said to them, "Peace be with you.""*

- *John 14:27 "Peace I leave with you; my peace I give you. I do not give to you as the world gives. Do not let your hearts be troubled and do not be afraid."*

- *John 16:33 "I have told you these things, so that in me you may have peace. In this world you will have trouble. But take heart! I have overcome the world."*

And the apostle Paul knew about peace that comes from closeness to Christ.

- *Philippians 4:7 "And the peace of God, which transcends all understanding, will guard your hearts and your minds in Christ Jesus."*

- *Colossians 3:15 "Let the peace of Christ rule in your hearts, since as members of one body you were called to peace. And be thankful."*

- *2 Thessalonians 3:16 "Now may the Lord of peace himself give you peace at all times and in every way. The Lord be with all of you."*

Choose at least one of today's verses and memorize it. Keep it close to your heart and pull it out whenever you need it.

WEEK FIVE RECAP
Hannah At Peace

Learn Anything?

Hannah found peace after she prayed from deep in her soul. God has a way of letting us know that he hears us. Maybe that is the definition of peace in a way: knowing God hears.

Hannah was able to keep her promise to God and that made her feel good, too. She expressed great joy in her song of thanks and praise. If you want peace, try prayer and praise. It worked for Hannah; it will work for you.

Talk About It...

1. Why does God answer some prayers and delay on others? Why do some people get what they pray for and others don't?

2. Have you ever prayed and it seemed that God didn't hear for a long time, and then one day everything fell into place? Will you thank Him for that now?

3. If you had been the parent of this child of your dreams, would you have been able to leave him at the temple and return home, trusting that he would be properly cared for by the priest? Why?

4. Is it important to teach small children how to worship God? Why or why not?

5. How do you feel when you have fulfilled a promise? How do you describe the feeling you get when with God's help you have done exactly what you set out to do?

WEEK FIVE RECAP
Hannah At Peace

MUSIC CHALLENGE

Listen To It...

Walking on Sunshine

Happy -- Pharrell Williams

Thank You, Jesus -- Hillsong United

It is Well With My Soul -- old hymn

Reactions:

_____

_____

_____

_____

Act On It...

1. The next time you are filled with joy and gratitude over God's blessings, sing your favorite happy song! Tell people why you are happy. Give God the credit.

2. Choose to memorize at least one of Day Five's verses about peace. Keep it close to your heart and pull it out whenever you need it.

Dear Lord, Thank you for the gift of peace.
I promise to look for it while keeping my eyes on you. The more I get to know you,
the more I feel your love and your peace. Thank you, God. Amen.

WEEK SIX
Hearing God's Voice in the Midst of Chaos

"Then He said, "Go out and stand on the mountain before the Lord." And behold, the Lord passed by, and a great and strong wind tore into the mountains and broke the rocks in pieces before the Lord, but the Lord was not in the wind; and after the wind an earthquake, but the Lord was not in the earthquake; and after the earthquake a fire, but the Lord was not in the fire; and after the fire a still small voice."

— 1 Kings 19:11-12

As promised, when Hannah felt the time had come, she left Samuel with Eli at the temple.

She entrusted Samuel to God's care knowing that the influence of Eli's corrupt sons might cause Samuel to turn away. She returned home. Though distant, she prayed for Samuel and sent new handmade clothes every year.

Samuel did his best to serve God in the temple. Amid the chaos of dishonest and immoral temple practices, Samuel heard God calling him in the night. Samuel remained faithful for life.

Dear Lord, my world is sometimes chaotic. My family, my community, even my church sometimes seem crazy to me. When I don't know who has the truth, Lord, I will turn to you and listen for your still, small voice. You alone are righteous and true and you love me more than anyone in this world. Amen.

Day One: Hophni and Phinehas

Have you ever had a bad teacher in a subject you love? What was that like?

_____

You struggle to learn anything. Maybe you decide you don't want to major in that subject after all.

Sometimes the teacher is OK but others in class are so disruptive that everyone is distracted. This is what happened to young Samuel at his 'school.'

After his parents returned to Ramah, Samuel lived and worked at the Temple under the supervision of Eli the priest. It must have been hard for Hannah to leave the little guy there, knowing the reputation of the priest and his sons.

Priestly duties included assisting pilgrims with required annual sacrifices described in Leviticus. There was a grain offering, a drink offering, a burnt offering and others. Meat from sheep or goats was cooked, usually boiled, the fat burned off on the altar. The burning fat's aromatic smoke rose toward heaven. It was as if the faithful were offering God a taste of the sacrifice.

The priests assisted with this process and they had the right to consume a portion of the cooked meat.

Read 1 Samuel 2:11-17.

How would you describe the actions of Eli's sons?

_____

Who were Eli's sons really serving?

_____

Sometimes the very people leading religious institutions are hollow and self-centered. Their actions speak of self-gratification, not devotion to God. When church leaders fail, many people become totally turned off. You may have heard of some of these scandals on the news. TV evangelist Jim Bakker was caught in extramarital relations and money skimming in the 1980s. American Roman Catholic priests were involved in child abuse and cover-up over several decades.

When adults have been deceived by these deceivers they often "throw their 'faith baby' out with the bathwater" so to speak. Their faith is tied to the leader and when the leader fails, their faith is crushed.

Imagine impressionable young Samuel watching Eli's sons. What was he learning? How did he manage to remain unaffected?

God is far more faithful and reliable than we humans are. God doesn't ask us to put our faith in imperfect people; he wants us to trust and believe in Him.

If someone who taught you to love Jesus was later caught in serious sin, would you allow it to affect your faith in God? Do you think God can be trusted to guide us even when our religious environment is not top-notch?

Day Two: Loving From Afar

Would you leave your child with a man whose sons were such awful examples?

_____

And what about Eli? Was he going to be any better guiding Samuel than he had been with his own sons, Phinehas and Hophni?

A faithful mother like Hannah probably had serious reservations about leaving little Samuel in the care of Eli and his miserable sons. If I were Hannah, I probably would have asked God if he wanted me to find another temple, or another school, or maybe even homeschool little Samuel for a while longer. I surely would not want these corrupt spiritual leaders to corrupt my child.

But Hannah knew God. She trusted God completely and she meant to keep her promise to him. She knew he listened to her and she trusted him to watch over her boy.

In our dangerous world, your parents may worry that they cannot be with you 24/7. Your mom no doubt prays that God will protect you. You are sometimes unavoidably left in situations where worldly or sinful influences might reach you. Without a deep trust in the Lord, this would be stressful for your parents at best and consuming at worst.

Hard as it was to leave her son at the temple for personalized training, Hannah did not forget Samuel.

Read 1Samuel 2:18-21.

What did Hannah do?

_____

A mother can never forget her children. She loves them even when they are not nearby.

Our three children are now grown and out of the house. One daughter recently married a wonderful man. The others are busy with work and school, so we don't see them all the time. They live in other parts of the country. Yet I think of them and wonder what I can do for them to show my love.

Look up these verses about a mother's love:

1Thessalonians 2:7   How does a mother care for her little children?

_____

Isaiah 49:15 What is the answer to the rhetorical question, "Can a mother forget her child?"

_____

Now read Psalm 113. How does this Psalm speak of the joy Hannah was feeling?

_____

_____

Samuel ministered before the Lord under Eli the priest according to 1Samuel 2:11.

What kinds of activities might that have included?

Maybe he was asked to keep the oil lamps lighted. Maybe he fed the animals or did other household-type chores. Maybe he learned to play an instrument so he could make music in the temple. Perhaps he learned to read the Torah. In any case, he stayed right there in the temple, in the house of God, a solemn place, a spiritual place, in spite of Eli's delinquent sons.

When my children were young, they loved the quiet church sanctuary on weekdays after mom's Bible study. I told them this was God's house, and they always wanted to stop in for a visit.

What kinds of worship activities have you done in your church as a child or youth? What has it meant to you? Will you look for a way to honor God in worship?

God speaks directly to children in ways adults are perhaps too 'smart' to understand. When children take on responsibilities in the house of God, they get close to God and his Spirit can speak to them. Serving as acolytes, singing in choirs, playing instruments are several ways to do this.

If a sailboat is to move, it must put its sail up to catch the wind, so the wind can move it forward.

Read 1Samuel 2:21b and 26 and 1Samuel 3:19.

How did Samuel grow up?

_____

Just for fun, look up Luke 2:52 and compare the description of young Jesus to the verses we just read about Samuel.

What similarities did you notice?

_____

What better description of a faithful young person than to "grow in stature and in favor with the Lord and with men."

We will see that Samuel's ministry was a lot like Jesus's.

How is service in worship like putting up your sail so the Holy Spirit can propel your faith?

Day Three: Consequences Foretold

Read 1Samuel 2: 22-24.

What did Eli do when he heard about his sons' bad behavior?

_____

He asked them why they took advantage of the people. He told them they were sinning against the Lord and he could not intercede. Eli seemed unable to control his sons. His rebuke was probably too little, too late.

God is patient with us, and forgives our mistakes over and over. But if we take God's mercy for granted and willfully continue doing wrong, God may lift his protective hand. Sadly, this was the case for Eli's wicked sons and eventually Eli and his entire family.

When your parents speak to you about something they see you doing, or an attitude they want to correct, how do you respond?

An unnamed prophet spoke to Eli in 1Samuel 2:27-36. The situation was so bad that God changed his mind on a promise he had made (verse 30) There are very few times in scripture that God changes his mind.

When individuals are entrusted with leadership in the church, God does not tolerate overt rejection of God's ways.

Read 1 Sam 2: 27-33.

How does the unnamed prophet begin his speech?

❏ "Here's what I think."

❏ "This is what the Lord says."

❏ "This is what people are saying."

What two questions does the prophet ask in Verse 29?

1)_____

2)_____

Eli, along with his sons, was guilty of scorning God's sacrifice, taking a gluttonous share of the meat. The sons also dishonored God by assaulting women near the temple entrance. Eli had rebuked them, but did not hold them to account.

What does the prophet foresee in verse 31?

_____

And in verse 32, what sadness is foretold?

_____

According to verse 33, how will the entire household die?

___ disease ___accident ___violence by sword

Specifically what coincidence will mark the deaths of Hophni and Phinehas?

_____

Can you imagine listening to such a dire warning? It must have been hard for Eli to hear.

I wonder if his wayward sons were listening. And what about Samuel? Do you think he overheard the message?

If Samuel heard this, what might he have been thinking or feeling?

_____

_____

Eli probably didn't sleep well after that dark warning. No doubt he began to wonder if there was anything he could do to alter his destiny and that of his sons.

Can you ask God to forgive you again and again for the same sins if you don't ever try to stop?

What does it really mean to repent?

Day Four: The Faithful Priest

In 1 Sam 2: 35-36, the unnamed prophet speaks of raising up a 'faithful priest" to replace the entire priestly family of which Eli was part. Who might this be? I wonder if Samuel would fill this role as an adult.

Eventually, when the time was right, God sent his own son, Jesus, to be our ultimate faithful high priest. The writer of Hebrews describes Jesus this way:

"For this reason he had to be made like them, fully human in every way, in order that he might become a merciful and faithful high priest in service to God, and that he might make atonement for the sins of the people. Because he himself suffered when he was tempted, he is able to help those who are being tempted." Heb 2:17-18

And in 1Peter 2:9-10, Peter describes the priesthood of all believers.

"But you are a chosen people, a royal priesthood, a holy nation, God's special possession, that you may declare the praises of him who called you out of darkness into his wonderful light. Once you were not a people, but now you are the people of God; once you had not received mercy, but now you have received mercy."

Each of us has some responsibility since we are part of the priesthood of all believers. Are you praising God for his wonderful mercy and showing that mercy to others?

If you consider yourself a believer, what can you take from the unnamed prophet's speech to Eli?

Are you a "faithful priest" in this generation?

Day Five: A Calling in the Night

In spite of Eli's family chaos, Samuel persevered. He continued 'ministering before the Lord.'

One night, Samuel awoke to a voice calling his name.

Read 1Sam 3:1-10.

Have you ever heard God calling you?

_____

Think for a minute about the conditions in Samuel's life when he heard this voice. He was at rest, quiet, not running from place to place or exhausted from sports and schoolwork. He was in the house of the Lord, serving him as he was taught. He was not following the bad examples of Eli's sons. He was attentive.

How does Samuel's situation compare to yours? Do you have a regular quiet time in which you listen for God? Are you distracted by peers who seem to get a lot of attention for their misdeeds? Are you serving the Lord in your own ways in your daily life?

At first, Samuel thought Eli must be calling him. After all, who else would be calling him in the middle of the night?

It takes practice to discern when God is speaking to us. We might make the same mistake Samuel did. Yet it was the Lord.

How old was Samuel at this time? Perhaps he was your age. What would you have done?

_____

1 Kings 19 tells the story of Elijah running for his life, very much afraid. He even prays that he will die, saying, " I have had enough, Lord, Take my life." Then he falls asleep. He is awakened twice by angels and told that the Lord will pass by. God spoke to Elijah when he passed by.

Read 1Kings 19: 11-12.

What was the sound of God's voice like?

❏ a great and powerful wind

❏ an earthquake

❏ a fire

❏ a gentle whisper

Modern skeptics mock the idea of hearing God's voice. It is not like a human voice, yet it is a voice we hear in our minds. It really speaks to us and we are foolish to disregard it.

But beware, not all voices you hear in your mind are of God. You must listen carefully. God will not tell you to do something that is not in his nature. By learning more about God from the Bible, you will understand his character and be able to discern his directions.

Other Bible characters have heard from God and wondered if it was real. Gideon, (in Judges 6) asked for confirmation… and then he asked again… he wasn't too sure. But he wanted to hear from God and he did.

Are you struggling to know what to do about a problem or relationship?

Are you running from something that seems to be nipping at your heels like Elijah was? Can you sit down, rest, and listen?

Find a way to get still before God and start praying. Ask God to speak to you. Ask for his guidance, or comfort, or specific direction.

Samuel continued to hear from God.

Read 1 Samuel 3: 19-21. How did God reveal himself to Samuel?

_____

Are you procrastinating? Not doing the one thing you know you are supposed to be doing? Can you get quiet and listen for the way forward?

As Britt Merrick says, in his book, *GodSpeed*, listening for God's direction is partly trial and error. You have to learn what his voice sounds like; what is his direction and what is not.

I believe God wants nothing more than to have our ready hearts listening for him. Prayer is not just listening to your own voice. It is learning to listen for God's.

Look up and copy Psalm 46:10.

_____

_____

Ask God for something specific or for a sign confirming something you think he wants you to do.

Pray the same prayer for a few days or a week and see what happens. God may not answer you in this short time, but he will surely answer in His time. Share results with your study group or with a close friend.

MUSIC CHALLENGE

"Here I am, Lord." Is a hymn we sing often in my church. It talks of hearing God calling in the night. Listen to it or find it in your hymn book. What is it saying to you?

WEEK SIX RECAP
Hearing God's Voice in the Midst of Chaos

Learn Anything?

There are two things to learn from this week's study. One is about keeping ears open for God. Like Samuel, we want to be able to hear God calling us, guiding us, teaching us. The world we live in can be very distracting. Prayer helps. The other thing to learn is that there are consequences for disrespecting God. Eli's sons didn't get that. When someone corrects you in love, you are wise to pay attention. God is merciful, but also righteous.

Talk About It...

1. If someone who taught you to love Jesus was later caught in serious sin, would you allow it to affect your faith in God? Do you think God can be trusted to guide us even when our religious environment is not top-notch?

2. How is service in worship like "putting up your sail" to catch the Holy Spirit?

3. When your parents speak to you about something they see you doing, or an attitude they want to correct, how do you respond?

4. What does it really mean to repent?

5. Are you a "faithful priest" in this generation?

6. Do you have a regular quiet time in which you listen for God?

WEEK SIX RECAP
Hearing God's Voice in the Midst of Chaos

MUSIC CHALLENGE

Listen To It...

                            Here I Am, Lord --

Reactions:

_____

_____

_____

_____

Act On It...

1. What kinds of worship activities have you done in your church as a child or youth? Can you look for a new way to honor God in worship?

2. Find a way to get still before God and start praying. Ask God to speak to you. Ask for his guidance, or comfort, or specific direction.

3. Ask God for something specific or for a sign confirming something you think he wants you to do. Pray the same prayer for a few days or a week and see what happens. God may not answer you in this short time, but he will surely answer in His time.

Share results with your study group or with a close friend.

Lord, forgive me when I busy myself with everything else
and put off listening to you. Amen.

WEEK SEVEN
Samuel, Hannah's Godly Son

"For I know the plans I have for you, declares the Lord, plans for welfare and not for calamity to give you a future and a hope." — Jeremiah 29:11

"Many are the plans in the human heart, but it is the Lord's purpose that prevails." --Proverbs 19:21

Living up to the expectations of parents and teachers is hard. Sometimes the pressure is great to be a leader, to always do the right thing. Often we don't get the chance to do the very thing we feel called to.

Hannah wanted Samuel to be devoted to God his whole life. God wanted Samuel to be his prophet in a time of transition.

In spite of the chaos around him, Samuel heard God's call and paid attention. He stepped into the role carefully, relying on God every step of the way.

*Dear God, I don't yet know what my life will bring.
Just as Samuel did what you asked of him, help me to follow,
one step at a time, so your purposes will be fulfilled. Amen*

Day One: Taking a Leadership Role

A good leader acts honorably, cares deeply for the people following, and points everyone to God. In 1 Samuel 7, Samuel took the leadership role in the way God intended. Notice what Samuel did as he stepped up to lead the people. Identify the verses in which he did these things:

He called for repentance.   verse_____

He united the people.   verse_____

He prayed and interceded for them. verse_____

He sacrificed appropriately. verse_____

He built a memorial.   verse_____

What do you notice about Samuel's first steps as leader?

_____

With an excellent leader/intercessor like Samuel in charge, why did Israel crave a king?

Read 1 Samuel 8: 1-5.

The people saw that other nations, which seemed more powerful, had one thing they didn't have: a king. They figured that to be powerful and respected they needed a king, too. What is the danger of thinking this way?

_____

They also noticed that Samuel's sons were not living up to their father's high standards.

What kind of judges were Samuel's sons?

_____

So when the elders gathered at Ramah, what reasons did they give for wanting a king?

_____
_____

How does it happen that the children of great leaders sometimes do not follow the pattern set by their parents?

The next verse, 1 Samuel: 8:6; is a great reminder for any leader.

Samuel felt _____.   So he _____.

Does that remind you of anyone else? Like maybe Samuel's mother, Hannah?

Pray about a disappointment in your life. Tell God how you feel. Listen for an answer.

As you read the rest of 1Samuel 8, notice God's encouraging words to Samuel.

"It's not you they are rejecting, but me.... Just like they always have."

God cared about Samuel's feelings. And he cares about yours, too.

Day Two: Earthly Kingdom or God's Kingdom

You know the saying, "Be careful what you wish for."

Having that big house or car may seem like great fun, but once you own it, you discover how much time and money is necessary to maintain it. Wise people weigh the pros and cons beforehand, because there is a down side to most everything.

God gave Samuel some insight about the potential pitfalls of earthly kingdoms, and asked him to tell the people.

What were some of the things he mentioned in

1 Samuel 8:10-18?

_____

_____

_____

These are the dangers of tyranny.

In a dictatorship, freedoms are exchanged for the "security" of knowing you have a mighty king. The next thousand years of Israel's history proved one thing beyond doubt: having an earthly king is no guarantee of prosperity or national security.

Why do we not heed the warnings God gives us? Do we have to learn everything the hard way? Is it the same with parental warnings?

Read 1Samuel 8:19-20.

What was the peoples' response, even after the warnings?

_____

After the people told Samuel they still wanted a king, what did God say in 1 Samuel 8:21-22?

_____

_____

God gave the warning but then instructed Samuel to find them a king anyway.

Why do you think he did that?

_____

When a toddler is learning to walk, falls are inevitable. Parents don't constantly hold a child's hand to keep the child from ever falling.

Likewise, God allowed the people to have a king, knowing there would be trouble.

Perhaps God wanted to teach us through experience the great difference between a worldly king and a heavenly one, so that one day we would appreciate the Kingdom of God so much more.

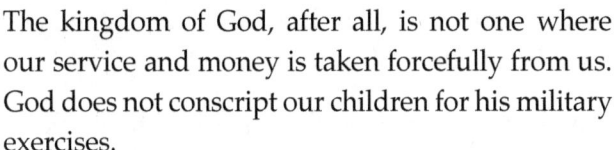

What does this phrase from the Lord's Prayer mean to you:

"Thy kingdom come, on earth as it is in heaven."

The kingdom of God, after all, is not one where our service and money is taken forcefully from us. God does not conscript our children for his military exercises.

In God's kingdom love wins all the time. We serve willingly out of gratitude, and receive love continually.

All people are loved equally and showered with mercy and grace.

God's kingdom cannot be conquered by any earthly army and does not depend on force.

One day we will stop wanting to "be like the other nations" and will strive only for God's kingdom to be made real on earth.

Who is your King?

For something extra -

Look up and read the sermon by Dr. S. M. Lockeridge entitled, "That's My King." He delivered this sermon in Detroit in 1976.

Day Three: Finding a King

Samuel kept his eyes open and his heart God-tuned as he looked for the first king of Israel.

Chapter 9 of 1 Samuel recounts a most unlikely story. Even the most imaginative Hollywood script writers probably would not have dreamed up this turn of events. It involved Saul's search for his father's wandering donkeys and his serendipitous meeting with Samuel. When Samuel met Saul, he recognized the man God intended for the first king.

Read 1 Samuel 9:15-17 and 1 Samuel 10: 1, and 1Samuel 10:9-11.

Who chose Saul to be king?

_____

Who anointed him?

_____

Who changed Saul's heart?

_____

Samuel anointed Saul king of Israel, but Saul had no clue why. At first he questioned Samuel's judgment: "Am I not a Benjamite from the smallest clan of the smallest tribe of Israel? Why do you say such a thing to me? (1Samuel 9:21)

And when the day came to publicly announce the new king, where was Saul hiding?

Read 1 Samuel 10:17-27 to find out.

_____

Have you ever wanted to hide instead of taking on the job you are called to do?

What physical attribute of Saul is mentioned in 1Samuel 10:23 and also in 9:2?

_____

So Saul was tall. A tall king is good, right? Everyone can look up to him. In his reign of 42 years, Saul did some good things. The Spirit of God enabled him to prophesy and guided him in some critical battles. His son Jonathan was also a mighty warrior.

However, Saul's ego got the best of him. Before long he became impatient for Samuel, who alone had authority to preside over ceremonial sacrifices. Samuel could see that Saul was unrepentant, and called him out in 1 Samuel 13:13-14.

Another time, Samuel instructed Saul to attack the Amalekites and destroy every one. Saul did not do it.

Read 1 Samuel 15:10-12.

What was God's reaction?

_____

What had Saul done before Samuel got there?

_____

Either Saul was totally incompetent as a warrior king or he was simply disobedient to the Lord who gave him power.

Whichever it was, he dug himself in deeper when he twisted the story to make himself look good. Saul claimed the reason he did not destroy the best cattle was to concoct a really good burnt sacrifice to God. But of course that is not what God had told him to do.

Read 1 Sam 15: 22-23.

How could this rebuke be for us as well?

Have you ever tried to make up for something you did wrong by a showy display of generosity?

Is it possible that all our church-going and money-giving will be found worthless because we did not obey the call of God on our lives?

Although it was not the end of his kingship, 1Samuel 15:26-28 marks the end of Saul's favor as God's anointed.

What did Samuel say to Saul in verse 28?

> "The Lord has _____ the kingdom of Israel from you today and has given it to _____ _____."

Read 1 Samuel 15:35.

What did Samuel do for Saul until the day he died?

_____

And how did God feel about making Saul king?

_____

Day Four: Time For a New King

God was sorry he had made Saul king. This man was not becoming the leader God and Samuel had hoped for. But he was not impeached or deposed immediately. He kept the kingship while Samuel searched for a new king.

Samuel may have felt like a failure in the "select-a-king" department. According to 1Samuel 15:35, he grieved over Saul. Samuel's work was not done. God already had another king in mind, and he commissioned Samuel to anoint him.

Read 1 Samuel 16: 1-5.

Where was Jesse from?

❏ Shiloh   ❏ Kiriath-Jearim

❏ Bethlehem   ❏ Ashdod

God had selected one of Jesse's sons to be the next king. Samuel would have to discern which one.

Read 1 Samuel 16: 7-13.

Who was Jesse's youngest son?

_____

Why was he not with the rest of the family when Samuel visited?

David was the youngest and the smallest of Jesse's sons. He was a shepherd. While out in the wilderness, he learned to take care of himself and the sheep. He killed wild animals with his slingshot and played his harp to pass the time. He had lots of time to think about God. No one paid much attention to him until Samuel stopped by.

CHEW ON THIS

When you are treated unfairly after serving well and doing a good job, to whom do you turn?

How did Samuel know David was the one?

_____

Much like young Samuel in service to the ineffective priest Eli, young David suddenly found himself in service to the out-of-favor King Saul.

Read 1Samuel 16:18-23.

What were David's first duties?

_____

_____

What was Saul struggling with?

_____

1Samuel 17 contains the well-loved story of David and Goliath. The whole chapter is worth a full reading.

Read these verses and judge the level of David's faith in God:

1 Samuel 17: 37 and 1 Samuel 17: 45-47.

❏ weak   ❏ tentative   ❏ strong and confident

You may already know how this battle ended. David became famous throughout the land when he killed Goliath. Jonathan, Saul's son, became David's best friend. Saul grew jealous and hateful toward David, even seeking to kill him multiple times.

Imagine how David felt when the king he served turned on him. All the good and courageous things he had done went unrewarded. Shouldn't Saul have been grateful for David?

David didn't turn his heartbreak into revenge. Just as Hannah turned to God in prayer, David did as well.

David was not perfect, but he eventually became the greatest earthly king Israel ever had.

Day Five: Hannah's Prayer Legacy

This is our last day together, so let's review.

Our study began with a look at Hannah's tough family situation. What do you think was the toughest thing about Hannah's life from what we learned?

_____

What, if anything, is the toughest thing about your family life?

_____

We studied Hannah's triangular marriage with Elkanah, her husband, and Peninnah, her "co-wife." She had to deal with merciless bullying, childlessness, and a husband who perhaps babied her with too much food. What physical or psychological problems accompanied all this?

_____

Hannah had few alternatives. As a practicing Jewish woman, she could not reasonably leave her marriage, nor did she want to. Elkanah loved her. Nor could she insist that Peninnah leave. She could not attend Weight Watchers or seek counseling for depression. She had no fertility treatment options as women do today.

Hannah did, however, have free access to the same God who is there for you today.

When she came unhinged, what did Hannah do?

_____

Looking back from the later years of Samuel's life, Hannah's prayer holds the key to some crucial years in the history of God's people.

If Hannah had NOT come unhinged and prayed, and God had NOT given her a son, and she had NOT kept her promise, think about how Israel's history might have been different.

Use your imagination.

God heard Hannah's prayer. Then he gave her a son, knowing she would keep her vow.

Her example of trust in the one true God was a giant witness to all around her.

Samuel matured knowing the love of his mother and the personal call of God on his life. He became the liaison between God and the first kings of Israel.

Samuel's prophetic career surely made Hannah proud. Samuel's discernment of God's spirit finally led to David's anointing as king. Israel prospered under King David. Three thousand years later we still benefit from David's creative writing.

Think about this:
Israel's history hinged on Hannah's prayer.

David wrote most of the Psalms in the Bible. David's songs are prayers, deep expressions of human emotions.

Read some of the following verses from the Psalms.

Circle some that closely express your feelings on something in your life right now.

                    Joy.........Psalm 81: 1-2, Psalm 95: 1-7

                    Sorrow........Psalm 116: 1-8

                    Weakness......Psalm 61: 1-3,   62: 1-2

Depression....... Psalm 6; Psalm 69:1-5; Psalm 77; Psalm 102

                    Slandered and afraid.......... Psalm 56

                    Fearful of violence or abuse....... Psalm 55: 4-11

                    Feeling bullied......Psalm 54: 1-4; Psalm 55: 1-3; Psalm 57

                    Needing forgiveness.........Psalm 51: 1-4

                    Envy/Jealousy..............Psalm 73: 2-3

                    Praise/thankfulness......... Psalm 66: 16-20

                    Confidence in God......... Psalm 23

Find one Psalm that you might need when you are disappointed, sad, or afraid and memorize it.

WEEK SEVEN RECAP
Samuel, Hannah's Godly Son

Learn Anything?

Samuel took God's call seriously. He listened for that voice he knew would guide him. He modeled great leadership and became the prophet who helped Israel transition from random leadership to a true earthly kingdom. God wants us to seek his kingdom first. When we think about Hannah's unhinged prayer, we realize that without it, the entire history of Israel might have been different. We never know how our prayers will affect others. Keep opening your heart to God.

Talk About It...

1. How does it happen that the children of great leaders sometimes mess up big-time?

2. Do we have to learn everything the hard way? Is it the same with parental warnings?

3. "Thy kingdom come, on earth as it is in heaven." What does this phrase from the Lord's Prayer mean to you?

4. Have you ever tried to make up for something you did wrong by a showy display of generosity?

5. When you are treated unfairly even when you have served well and done a good job, to whom do you turn?

6. How did Israel's history hinge on Hannah's decision to turn to God in prayer?

WEEK SEVEN RECAP
Samuel, Hannah's Godly Son

MUSIC CHALLENGE

Listen To It...

your favorite Christian song

Sometimes By Step -- Rich Mullins

Reactions:

_____

_____

_____

_____

Act On It...

1. Pray about a disappointment in your life. Tell God how you feel. Listen for an answer.

2. Who is your King? How do you know?

3. Look up and read the sermon by Dr. S. M. Lockeridge, delivered in Detroit in 1976, entitled "That's My King."

4. Find one Psalm that you might need in a situation of disappointment or fear or sorrow and memorize it.

Dear Lord, thank you for showing me that you know what I am going through.
I am so glad the Bible preserved the prayers and songs of people like me
who had tough times too.
Help me always remember I can pour out my heart to you, my King, in prayer. Amen

THANK YOU

Thank you for joining me in this study of Hannah and her godly son, Samuel.

I hope you learned how even through the pain you can always turn directly to God. He loves you and wants to answer your prayers. You never know how God might use you. God's answer to Hannah's prayer helped not only her own sadness, but it also paved the way for Israel to become a kingdom and for David to reign as a great poet and king. David would eventually produce offspring that would ultimately parent Jesus, God's own son and the ultimate King of Kings.

Take a minute to thank God for the way he works and ask him for whatever you need. He is waiting to hear from you, no matter what you are going through. If you ever feel you are coming 'unhinged,' take time to pour out your heart to God like Hannah did.

Then see what He will do.

I'll be praying for you.

Sherree

**OTHER TEEN BIBLE STUDIES
By Sherree G. Funk**

Order these great studies at BibleStudiesforTeens.com or Amazon.com

Lydia of Philippi: Believer in the Lord   ISBN 978-0-9823137-3-2
    A guided Bible study of Acts 16 and Paul's letter to the Philippians

Joshua: Strong and Courageous   ISBN 978-0-9823137-1-8
    A guided Bible study for teens from Exodus, Numbers, Deuteronomy, and Joshua

Ruth and Boaz: Woman of Excellence, Man of Honor ISBN 978-0-9823137-2-5
    A guided Bible study of Ruth and Proverbs 31

Peter: Rock Star from Galilee   ISBN 978-0-9823137-6-3   (also available as an e-book)
    A guided Bible study for teens and adults

www.ingramcontent.com/pod-product-compliance
Lightning Source LLC
Chambersburg PA
CBHW060518300426
44112CB00017B/2722